UNDERSTANDING BORDERLINE PERSONALITY DISORDER

A Comprehensive Guide to Recognizing, Coping with, and Healing from BPD

Betty K. Cobb

Table of Contents

Chapter 1

<u>UNDERSTANDING PERSONALITY DISORDERS</u>

Personality disorders are a category of mental health diseases defined by persisting patterns of thoughts, feelings, and behavior that differ markedly from social norms and expectations. These behaviors are firmly rooted and frequently create unhappiness and damage in different aspects of life, including relationships, jobs, and general functioning.

Understanding personality disorders is vital for people, families, and mental health professionals as it may assist demystify these complicated problems and lead to appropriate treatment methods.

<u>OVERVIEW OF PERSONALITY DISORDERS</u>

There are 10 forms of personality disorders. They are organized into three separate types called clusters. Personality disorders are divided into three groups in the Diagnostic and Statistical Manual of Mental Disorders (DSM-5): Cluster A (odd or eccentric disorders), Cluster B (dramatic, emotional, or erratic disorders), and Cluster C (anxious or scared disorders).

Cluster A Personality Disorders

Cluster A personality disorders include Paranoid Personality Disorder, Schizoid Personality Disorder, and Schizotypal Personality Disorder. Paranoid Personality Disorder is defined by a chronic suspicion and suspiciousness of others, leading to an abiding assumption that others are attempting to mislead, exploit, or hurt them.

Schizoid Personality Disorder is defined by a detachment from social connections, restricted emotional expression, and a predilection for solitary hobbies. Schizotypal Personality Disorder entails unusual ideas, quirky conduct, and difficulty with social and interpersonal connections.

Cluster B Personality Disorders

Cluster B personality disorders comprise Borderline Personality Disorder, Narcissistic Personality Disorder, Histrionic Personality Disorder, and Antisocial Personality Disorder. Borderline Personality Disorder is characterized by instability in self-image, relationships, and emotions, frequently leading to impulsive and self-destructive actions.

Narcissistic Personality Disorder entails a grandiose sense of self-importance, a need for praise, and a lack of empathy. Histrionic Personality Disorder is characterized by attention-seeking behavior, excessive emotionality, and a propensity to be excessively dramatic. Antisocial Personality Disorder is characterized by a disrespect for the rights and emotions of others, a lack of remorse, and a practice of lying and manipulation.

Cluster C Personality Disorders

Cluster C personality disorders include Avoidant Personality Disorder, Dependent Personality Disorder, and Obsessive-Compulsive Personality Disorder. Avoidant Personality Disorder is a chronic pattern of social inhibition, feelings of inadequacy, and hypersensitivity to criticism, resulting in avoidance of social contact.

Dependent Personality Disorder is characterized by excessive dependence on others, a great fear of abandonment, and trouble making choices independently. Obsessive-Compulsive Personality Disorder entails an obsession with orderliness, perfectionism, and control, frequently leading to inflexible habits and difficulty in adjusting to change.

CAUSES AND DEVELOPMENT

Genetic predisposition may play a role, since some personality characteristics and temperaments may be inherited. Environmental variables such as early trauma, neglect, or inconsistent parenting may also contribute to the development of maladaptive patterns of behavior.

Additionally, some personality disorders may occur as a consequence of disturbances in brain structure and functioning, including anomalies in neurotransmitter systems and neural connections.

Causes of Borderline Personality Disorder (BPD)

Borderline Personality Disorder (BPD) is a complicated mental health illness with numerous origins. The specific reason has not been determined yet but It is thought that a mix of genetic, biochemical, environmental, and psychological variables contribute to the development of BPD.

Understanding the underlying reasons is critical for proper diagnosis, successful treatment, and giving appropriate support to those with BPD. Here, we dig into the numerous elements that are considered to have a role in the development of BPD:

1. **<u>Hereditary Factors:</u>** There is evidence to indicate that hereditary factors contribute to the vulnerability to BPD. Studies have revealed that persons with a family history of BPD or other linked mental health issues, such as mood disorders or drug use disorders, are at a greater risk of developing BPD. Genetic research is undertaken to uncover particular genes or genetic variants that may be connected with the illness.

2. <u>Neurobiological Factors:</u> Research has identified several neurobiological anomalies in persons with BPD. Brain imaging studies have identified variations in the structure and functioning of brain areas involved in emotion regulation, impulse control, and interpersonal processing.

For example, anomalies in the amygdala, prefrontal cortex, and hippocampus have been discovered, which may lead to emotional dysregulation and difficulty in social relationships.

3. <u>Environmental Factors:</u> a. Early Life Experiences: Adverse childhood events, including physical or sexual abuse, neglect, early loss or separation from caregivers, or inconsistent parenting, have been recognized as risk factors for developing BPD. These early life events may affect the development of emotional regulation abilities, attachment patterns, and the building of a solid sense of self.

b. **<u>Invalidating Environments:</u>** Growing up in an invalidating or invalidation-prone environment, when feelings and experiences are disregarded, ignored, or invalidated, might lead to the development of BPD. This includes occasions when a person's emotional reactions are persistently undercut or trivialized, resulting in difficulty in understanding and controlling emotions.

c. **<u>Family Dynamics:</u>** Chaotic family contexts, high levels of conflict, damaged attachment bonds, or inconsistent and unpredictable parenting techniques might contribute to the development of BPD. Unstable or abusive family dynamics may impair the individual's capacity to build healthy relationships, control emotions, and develop a solid sense of self.

4. <u>Psychological Factors:</u> a. Emotional Sensitivity and Reactivity: Individuals with

BPD generally demonstrate heightened emotional sensitivity and reactivity. They may feel emotions more vividly and have difficulties controlling these emotions efficiently. This emotional dysregulation may emerge as quick mood swings, extreme rage, and impulsivity.

b. **<u>Identity Disturbance:</u>** BPD is characterized by a fragile or unstable sense of self. Individuals with BPD may struggle with identity development and have issues sustaining a consistent self-image or sense of identity. This identity disruption may lead to feelings of emptiness, bewilderment, and a lack of a steady sense of purpose or direction in life.

c. **<u>Cognitive Factors:</u>** Cognitive biases and patterns of thinking linked with BPD, such as black-and-white thinking, idealization and devaluation, and negative self-perception, contribute to the maintenance of BPD symptoms. These cognitive distortions may alter the individual's image of themselves, others, and their relationships, further worsening emotional dysregulation and interpersonal issues.

It is vital to highlight that BPD does not have a single cause, and the interaction of various elements leads to its development. The specific processes and relationships between these elements are still being explored and understood.

Additionally, it is vital to note that not everyone with risk factors will acquire BPD, and persons without clear risk factors might nevertheless develop the disease.

By having full knowledge of the causes of BPD, mental health practitioners may modify treatment techniques to fit the unique requirements of people with the illness. Early intervention, counseling, and support that address the genetic, biological, environmental, and psychological elements may greatly improve outcomes and increase the quality of life for those with BPD.

People with personality disorders may have problems understanding that they have a problem. To them, such ideas are normal. They may perceive others as the issue. So they may not seek assistance when they need it. Or, if they seek therapy, it may be because of another reason.

They may be searching for therapy because of other mental health symptoms or troubles with relationships and jobs. Sometimes someone else, such as a family member or social agency, may urge them to receive assistance.

Diagnosing personality disorders may be problematic owing to the intricacy and overlap of symptoms. A full examination often incorporates a thorough clinician interview, self-report questionnaires, collateral information from family and friends, and a review of medical and mental history.

The DSM-5 criteria give guidance for diagnosing particular personality disorders based on the existence of persisting patterns of behavior and impairment in multiple aspects of life.

Understanding personality disorders is a complicated task that involves a detailed investigation of the many forms, causes, and treatment techniques. By expanding awareness and education about personality disorders, we may minimize stigma, encourage early intervention, and give effective support and treatment to persons living with these problems.

It is vital to remember that with the correct therapies and support, persons with personality disorders may have satisfying and meaningful lives.

Chapter 2

<u>INSIGHT INTO BORDERLINE PERSONALITY DISORDER</u>

Borderline Personality Disorder (BPD) is a mental health disease defined by a widespread pattern of instability in interpersonal interactions, self-image, and emotions.

Individuals with BPD generally exhibit significant emotional dysregulation, impulsivity, and problems sustaining stable relationships. The disease receives its name from the historical assumption that these people teetered on the "borderline" between neurotic and psychotic disorders.

People with BPD are typically on edge. They have high discomfort and fury levels, therefore they may be quickly offended. They struggle with ideas and attitudes about themselves and others, which may create unhappiness in many aspects of their life.

People living with BPD frequently have an overwhelming fear of instability and abandonment. As a consequence, people have trouble being alone.

The illness is also known for irritability, mood swings, and impulsiveness. These features might prevent individuals from being near someone with BPD. On top of this, many persons with the condition struggle with self-awareness and how others perceive them. This makes them incredibly sensitive.

BPD is a mental and bodily disorder. Its symptoms begin to show throughout the early teenage years and progressively improve during adult life.

The Diagnostic and Statistical Manual of Mental Disorders, Fifth Edition (DSM-5), published by the American Psychiatric Association, offers the definitive diagnostic criteria for Borderline Personality Disorder.

According to the DSM-5, the main characteristics of BPD include a persistent pattern of instability in self-image, interpersonal relationships, and emotion, combined with severe impulsivity that starts in early adulthood and is prevalent across diverse settings.

The DSM-5 provides nine criteria for diagnosing Borderline Personality Disorder, of which a person must fulfill at least five to earn the diagnosis. These requirements are as follows:

1. Frantic attempts to avert actual or imagined abandonment:
Individuals with BPD frequently suffer an acute fear of abandonment, driving them to

engage in frenzied actions to escape it. These behaviors may involve performing impulsive actions, such as self-harm, to elicit support or comfort from others.

2. Patterns of unstable and passionate interpersonal relationships:

Individuals with BPD usually struggle with creating and maintaining solid relationships. They may swing between idealizing and depreciating others, resulting in disputes and emotional instability.

3. Identity disruption and unsteady self-image:

BPD is related to considerable instability in self-image, self-identity, and values. Individuals may have an ambiguous sense of self, leading to feelings of emptiness and bewilderment about their objectives, values, and purpose in life.

4. Impulsivity in at least two potentially self-damaging areas:
Impulsivity is a basic aspect of BPD, and it displays in numerous ways, such as reckless spending, drug misuse, binge eating, dangerous sexual practices, or participating in self-harming behaviors.

5. Recurrent suicidal acts, gestures, threats, or self-harm:
Individuals with BPD typically suffer from self-harming activities, including cutting, burning, or other types of self-inflicted pain. They may also have recurring suicidal thoughts, engage in suicide gestures, or make threats of self-harm.

6. Affective instability:
Emotional dysregulation is a key hallmark of BPD. Individuals may suffer quick and strong mood swings, frequently driven by external events or perceived interpersonal rejection.

7. Chronic emotions of emptiness:
Individuals with BPD typically express a persistent sensation of emptiness and an inner vacuum, which they may seek to fill via impulsive actions, passionate relationships, or drug use.

8. Inappropriate and severe anger or trouble regulating anger:
Individuals with BPD usually struggle with anger control. They may have extreme, inappropriate anger responses, and they may find it tough to manage or control their anger.

9. Transient, stress-related paranoid ideation or severe dissociation symptoms:
BPD may be accompanied by short periods of paranoid thinking or dissociative experiences, especially in reaction to stressful conditions.

It is vital to remember that the intensity and particular symptoms of BPD might vary from person to person. Diagnosis and therapy should be undertaken by trained mental health specialists who can analyze the individual's symptoms, history, and general functioning.

The diagnosis of Borderline Personality Disorder includes a full examination of the individual's behavior, feelings, and interpersonal connections. A diagnosis should be made thoughtfully and with compassion, since it might have substantial ramifications for the individual's treatment and well-being.

Early detection and intervention, together with appropriate therapy techniques, may help persons with BPD enjoy more rewarding and secure lives.

RISK FACTORS OF BORDERLINE PERSONALITY DISORDER (BPD)

Borderline Personality Disorder (BPD) is a complicated mental health illness that may originate from a mix of genetic, environmental, and psychological factors.

While the specific origins of BPD are not completely known, some risk factors have been discovered. These risk factors raise the probability of getting BPD, however, they do not ensure the development of the illness. Understanding these risk factors may lead to early detection, intervention, and successful treatment of BPD.

1. Genetic Predisposition:

There is evidence to imply that there is a hereditary component to the development of BPD. Studies have revealed that persons with a family history of BPD or other linked mental health illnesses, such as mood disorders or drug use disorders, are at a higher risk of developing BPD themselves. However, it is vital to emphasize that genetics alone are not sufficient to create BPD, and other environmental and psychological variables play a substantial influence.

2. Early Childhood Experiences:

Childhood events and environmental variables have a key influence on the development of BPD. Adverse childhood events, including physical or sexual abuse, neglect, emotional trauma, or inconsistent parenting, may dramatically increase the chance of developing BPD.

These events may disturb healthy emotional and social development, resulting in challenges in emotion regulation, attachment disorders, and a damaged sense of self.

3. Invalidating Environments:

Growing raised in an invalidating or emotionally invalidating environment might contribute to the development of BPD. An invalidating environment is defined by a lack of empathy, understanding, and validation of an individual's feelings and experiences.

When emotional reactions are frequently disregarded, mocked, or ignored, people may internalize a feeling of invalidation, leading to emotional dysregulation and difficulty in controlling emotions successfully.

4. Neurobiological Factors:

Research shows that persons with BPD may have variations in brain anatomy and functioning. Neuroimaging studies have identified anomalies in regions of the brain involved in emotion regulation, impulse control, and interpersonal processing.

The imbalance of neurotransmitters, such as serotonin and dopamine, has also been linked with BPD. These neurological variables may contribute to the emotional dysregulation and impulsive behaviors typical of the condition.

5. Co-occurring Mental Health Conditions:

BPD commonly co-occurs with other mental health issues, such as mood disorders (e.g., depression, bipolar disorder), anxiety disorders, drug use disorders, and eating disorders.

The existence of these co-occurring illnesses might complicate the diagnosis and management of BPD. The shared risk factors and overlapping symptoms between BPD and other mental health problems imply a complicated interaction between them.

6. Environmental Factors:

Environmental stresses, such as significant life changes, interpersonal issues, or chronic stress, might contribute to the development or worsening of BPD symptoms. Traumatic situations, particularly physical or sexual assault, may further raise the chance of developing BPD.

7. Temperamental Factors:

Certain temperamental qualities, such as high sensitivity, impulsivity, and emotional intensity, may enhance the risk of developing BPD. These qualities, when paired with unpleasant life events or invalidating situations, may lead to the development of the illness.

It is crucial to emphasize that although these risk factors are connected with an increased possibility of developing BPD, they do not indicate the existence of the condition.

Many persons with these risk factors do not get BPD, while those without these risk factors may nevertheless develop the disease. BPD is a complicated disorder impacted by a variety of elements, and the interaction of heredity, environment, and psychological factors is unique for each person.

Early detection of risk factors and appropriate treatments, like therapy and support, may help lessen the effect of these variables and improve outcomes for persons at risk of or living with BPD. A full knowledge of the risk factors helps aid mental health practitioners in offering individualized treatment methods and support for persons with BPD.

<u>CO-OCCURRING MENTAL HEALTH CONDITIONS</u>

Borderline Personality Disorder (BPD) is typically accompanied by the presence of other mental health problems. These co-occurring diseases may complicate the diagnosis, treatment, and overall management of BPD.

Understanding the typical co-occurring mental health problems may assist mental health practitioners offer comprehensive treatment and improve outcomes for patients with BPD.

1. Mood Disorders:

Mood disorders, such as major depressive disorder and bipolar disorder, commonly co-occur with BPD. Individuals with BPD may suffer strong and fluctuating mood swings, which might mirror symptoms of mood disorders.

The emotional dysregulation characteristic of BPD might lead to the development or aggravation of depressed or manic symptoms. The existence of a mood illness with BPD may raise the risk of self-harm, suicidal thoughts, and overall impairment in functioning.

2. Anxiety Disorders:

Anxiety disorders typically co-occur with BPD, including generalized anxiety disorder (GAD), social anxiety disorder, and post-traumatic stress disorder (PTSD). Individuals with BPD typically endure continuous emotions of anxiety and concern.

The fear of abandonment, the need for ongoing reassurance, and the powerful emotions associated with BPD might lead to the development of anxiety disorders. The existence of anxiety disorders might further enhance mental suffering and impede an individual's capacity to deal with ordinary life pressures.

3. Substance Use Disorders:

Substance use disorders typically co-occur with BPD. Individuals with BPD may resort to drug use as a strategy to deal with emotional anguish, control their moods, or numb their powerful emotions. Substance usage may give a brief reprieve from the severe symptoms of BPD.

However, it may aggravate emotional dysregulation, impulsive behaviors, and general functioning. The co-occurrence of BPD and drug use disorders demands integrated treatment techniques that address both diseases concurrently.

4. Eating Disorders:

Eating disorders, such as anorexia nervosa, bulimia nervosa, and binge-eating disorder, usually co-occur with BPD. Both BPD and eating disorders have many symptoms, such as emotional dysregulation, impulsivity, and problems with self-image.

Individuals with BPD may engage in disordered eating practices as a method of managing their emotions or seeking a feeling of self-worth. The existence of both BPD and an eating problem needs specialist therapy that addresses the complicated interaction between these illnesses.

5. Dissociative Disorders:
Dissociative illnesses, including dissociative identity disorder and depersonalization-derealization disorder, may co-occur with BPD. Dissociation refers to a separation from one's ideas, emotions, memories, or sense of identity.

Individuals with BPD may develop dissociative symptoms as a reaction to traumatic events or as a technique to deal with overwhelming emotions. The occurrence of dissociative disorders with BPD may complicate therapy and necessitate specialist therapeutic measures.

6.   Attention-Deficit/Hyperactivity Disorder (ADHD):

ADHD is typically noticed in patients with BPD. ADHD is characterized by difficulty with concentration, impulse control, and hyperactivity. The impulsivity and emotional dysregulation found in BPD might overlap with symptoms of ADHD. Individuals with BPD and ADHD may struggle with focus, organization, and impulsivity, necessitating extensive treatment techniques that address both diseases.

7. Personality Disorders:

It is fairly unusual for persons with BPD to exhibit features or satisfy diagnostic criteria for other personality disorders. This overlap may make diagnosis and therapy more challenging. Common co-occurring personality disorders include narcissistic personality disorder, antisocial personality disorder, and avoidant personality disorder.

The presence of various personality disorders may aggravate challenges in interpersonal connections, self-identity, and general functioning. It is necessary to distinguish between the basic diagnosis of BPD and the existence of comorbid personality disorders to adapt treatment strategies successfully.

8. Post-Traumatic Stress Disorder (PTSD):

PTSD usually co-occurs with BPD, particularly in persons who have endured considerable trauma. Traumatic events, such as physical or sexual abuse, neglect, or witnessing violence, may contribute to the development of both BPD and PTSD.

The symptoms of BPD, including emotional dysregulation, impulsivity, and self-destructive behaviors, may be increased in persons with co-occurring PTSD. Treatment treatments for BPD and PTSD should address trauma-related symptoms and concentrate on stabilizing emotions and increasing overall well-being.

9. Obsessive-Compulsive Disorder (OCD):

OCD may co-occur with BPD, however, the link betwpeen the two is not well known. Individuals with BPD may display obsessive thoughts and engage in compulsive actions as a method of dealing with anxiety or intrusive thoughts. The existence of OCD plus BPD might complicate therapy and need a thorough strategy that addresses both diseases.

10. Self-Harm and Suicidal Behaviors:

While not a mental health disease per se, self-harm and suicide behaviors are serious problems typically connected with BPD. Extreme emotional dysregulation, fear of abandonment, and problems in controlling upsetting emotions may cause persons with BPD to engage in self-harming activities or have repeated thoughts of suicide.

These activities typically function as maladaptive coping methods to reduce emotional discomfort or acquire a feeling of control. Addressing self-harm and suicide behaviors involves a multifaceted strategy, including crisis management, safety planning, and long-term therapy treatments.

It is vital to understand that the existence of co-occurring mental health problems might complicate the diagnosis and management of BPD. Integrated and comprehensive treatment techniques that meet the distinctive requirements of each person are necessary for optimal management.

Treatment may require a mix of psychotherapy, medication, support groups, and psychosocial therapies targeted to the particular issues associated with both BPD and co-occurring illnesses.

Additionally, a comprehensive approach that incorporates the individual's strengths, resilience, and support networks may assist in long-term healing and increased quality of life. It is crucial to contact a qualified mental health practitioner to perform a complete evaluation and design a personalized treatment plan that addresses the complications of co-occurring mental health problems in persons with BPD.

Because borderline personality disorder is as distinctive as each individual who lives with it, therapy needs a specific approach.

Many individuals with BPD, at times, feel emotional agony from the disease. However, you don't have to succumb to living a life that's full of misery and heartache. It's vital to take care of yourself, know your triggers, and work with your healthcare team to establish what therapies will help keep it in control.

By committing to care and knowing as much as can about it, you can make a difference in your quality of life—and the lives of people around you.

Chapter 3

IMPACTS AND TRIGGERS OF BPD

Triggers of Borderline Personality Disorder (BPD)

Borderline Personality Disorder (BPD) is characterized by emotional dysregulation, impulsivity, and difficulties in interpersonal relationships. While the exact causes of BPD are not fully understood, certain triggers can exacerbate the symptoms and contribute to the onset of BPD episodes.

It is important to note that triggers can vary from person to person, and what may trigger one individual with BPD may not have the same effect on another. Understanding the common triggers can help individuals with BPD, as well as their loved ones and mental health professionals, anticipate and manage these triggers effectively.

1. Abandonment and Rejection:

One of the primary triggers for individuals with BPD is the fear of abandonment and rejection. Perceived or actual threats of abandonment, such as a relationship breakup or feeling excluded, can evoke intense emotional responses and escalate symptoms of BPD. The fear of being alone and the desire for constant reassurance and validation can contribute to intense anxiety, emotional turmoil, and impulsive behaviors.

2. Relationship Conflict:

Difficulties in maintaining stable and healthy relationships are a hallmark of BPD. Relationship conflicts, such as arguments, disagreements, or perceived criticisms, can trigger intense emotional reactions and contribute to a sense of rejection or abandonment. The inherent difficulties in regulating emotions and interpreting social cues may lead individuals with BPD to have heightened sensitivity to interpersonal conflicts, which can escalate into intense emotional episodes.

3. Traumatic Experiences:

Traumatic experiences, such as physical or sexual abuse, neglect, or witnessing violence, can serve as significant triggers for individuals with BPD. These traumatic events may be directly linked to the development of BPD or can exacerbate existing symptoms. Trauma can evoke intense emotional responses, trigger intrusive thoughts or memories, and disrupt an individual's ability to regulate emotions effectively.

4. Loss and Grief:

Experiences of loss, such as the death of a loved one, the end of a significant relationship, or the loss of a job, can be triggering for individuals with BPD. The intense emotions associated with grief and the challenges in adjusting to change can exacerbate symptoms of BPD. The feelings of emptiness, instability, and abandonment can be heightened during periods of loss and mourning.

5. Perceived Criticism or Rejection:

Individuals with BPD often have heightened sensitivity to perceived criticism or rejection. Even minor feedback or perceived slights can trigger intense emotional responses, leading to feelings of shame, self-doubt, and anger. The fear of being judged, rejected, or abandoned can intensify emotional dysregulation and impulsive behaviors.

6. Intense Emotional States:

Extreme emotions, such as anger, sadness, or anxiety, can act as triggers for individuals with BPD. Emotional dysregulation is a core feature of the disorder, and fluctuations between emotional extremes can occur rapidly. When faced with intense emotional states, individuals with BPD may struggle to effectively manage and regulate their emotions, leading to impulsive and self-destructive behaviors.

7. Feeling Overwhelmed or Overstimulated:

Overwhelming or overstimulating environments, such as crowded places, loud noises, or high-pressure situations, can trigger distress and escalate symptoms of BPD. Individuals with BPD may have difficulty processing sensory stimuli, leading to feelings of being overwhelmed or unable to cope. These situations can exacerbate emotional dysregulation and impulsive behaviors.

8. Personal Transitions or Change:

Transitions or changes in life circumstances, such as moving to a new place, starting a new job, or significant life events, can act as triggers for individuals with BPD. The inherent difficulties in adapting to change and the fear of the unknown can intensify emotional reactivity and instability. Individuals with BPD may struggle with a loss of routine or predictability, leading to increased distress and symptoms.

9.   Feeling   Misunderstood   or Invalidated:

Invalidation or a lack of understanding from others can trigger intense emotional reactions in individuals with BPD. When their emotions or experiences are dismissed, minimized, or invalidated, individuals with BPD may feel unheard, misunderstood, or rejected. This can exacerbate feelings of loneliness, emotional dysregulation, and interpersonal difficulties.

10. Substance Use or Withdrawal:

Substance use or withdrawal from substances can act as triggers for individuals with BPD. Substance use can temporarily alleviate distressing emotions or provide a sense of escape. However, it can intensify emotional dysregulation, impulsive behaviors, and overall instability. The withdrawal from substances can also trigger intense emotional responses and increase vulnerability to BPD episodes.

11. Perceived Abandonment:

Perceived abandonment can be just as triggering as actual abandonment for individuals with BPD. Even minor events or situations that trigger feelings of neglect or rejection can intensify emotional dysregulation and lead to impulsive behaviors. The fear of being abandoned can be pervasive and may manifest in clingy or dependent behaviors in relationships.

12. Intimate Relationships:

Intimate relationships can be particularly triggering for individuals with BPD due to the vulnerability and emotional closeness involved. The fear of intimacy, coupled with the fear of abandonment, can lead to heightened sensitivity and reactivity in romantic partnerships. The challenges of maintaining a stable and healthy relationship can contribute to relationship conflicts and emotional distress.

13. Negative Self-Image:

Individuals with BPD often struggle with a negative self-image and low self-esteem. Triggers that reinforce negative beliefs about themselves, such as criticism, failure, or perceived shortcomings, can intensify feelings of self-hatred, worthlessness, and despair. These triggers can contribute to self-destructive behaviors, including self-harm or suicidal ideation.

14. Feeling Emotionally Suffocated:

While the fear of abandonment is prevalent in individuals with BPD, there can also be a fear of engulfment or feeling emotionally suffocated in relationships. The perceived loss of personal boundaries or a sense of losing one's identity within a relationship can trigger intense emotional responses and result in attempts to regain a sense of autonomy.

15. Loneliness and Isolation:

Feelings of loneliness and isolation can act as significant triggers for individuals with BPD. The fear of being alone and the inherent difficulties in forming and maintaining stable relationships can contribute to a sense of disconnection and profound emotional pain. These triggers can lead to impulsive behaviors or attempts to seek attention and connection, even if it is unhealthy.

16. Stressful Life Events:

High levels of stress or significant life events, such as financial difficulties, job loss, or legal problems, can act as triggers for individuals with BPD. Stressful circumstances can amplify emotional dysregulation, increase impulsivity, and exacerbate symptoms of BPD. The lack of effective coping mechanisms during challenging times can intensify the impact of these triggers.

17. Lack of Structure or Routine:

A lack of structure or routine in daily life can be triggering for individuals with BPD. Without a clear framework or predictable schedule, individuals with BPD may feel a heightened sense of anxiety, uncertainty, and instability. Establishing a structured routine and engaging in activities that promote stability and a sense of purpose can help manage these triggers.

18. Criticism of Behaviors or Actions:

Criticism of behaviors or actions, even if well-intentioned, can trigger intense emotional reactions in individuals with BPD. They may interpret constructive feedback as a personal attack, leading to feelings of shame, anger, or defensiveness. It is important to provide feedback and support in a validating and compassionate manner to avoid triggering emotional distress.

It is crucial to recognize that triggers can vary from person to person and may change over time. Building self-awareness, developing coping strategies, and seeking professional support are essential for individuals with BPD to effectively manage and navigate triggers.

With the right tools and support, individuals with BPD can learn to identify and respond to triggers in healthier and more adaptive ways, leading to improved emotional well-being and overall functioning.

IMPACTS OF BPD

Borderline Personality Disorder (BPD) may have a tremendous influence on people's lives, as well as on their relationships, emotions, and general functioning. BPD is characterized by emotional dysregulation, impulsivity, identity issues, and difficulty in interpersonal interactions.

The impacts of BPD may be far-reaching, impacting all elements of an individual's life and well-being. Understanding the effect of BPD is vital for offering appropriate assistance and therapies to persons impacted by the condition.

1. Emotional Instability:

One of the distinguishing aspects of BPD is emotional dysregulation. Individuals with BPD frequently feel powerful and quickly fluctuating emotions, including rage, sorrow, anxiety, and emptiness.

These feelings may be overpowering and tough to regulate, resulting in impulsive actions, self-destructive inclinations, and frequent mood swings. The emotional instability might interfere with everyday functioning, relationships, and general quality of life.

2. Impulsive Behaviors:

Impulsivity is a basic component of BPD and may present in numerous ways. Individuals with BPD may engage in impulsive behaviors such as irresponsible spending, drug misuse, self-harm, hazardous sexual activities, or binge eating.

These spontaneous activities frequently serve as a strategy to manage emotions or seek instant respite from suffering. However, they may have significant effects, including bodily injury, legal troubles, financial instability, and ruined relationships.

3. Unstable Relationships:

Difficulties in interpersonal connections are a typical feature of BPD. Individuals with BPD may battle with significant feelings of abandonment, have a heightened sensitivity to perceived rejection, and face challenges in forming and sustaining solid relationships.

The fear of desertion may lead to clinging or dependent behaviors, whereas emotional reactivity and impulsivity can result in frequent disagreements and chaotic dynamics. The instability and conflict inside partnerships may lead to emotional suffering and further prolong the cycle of unstable relationships.

4. Identity Disturbance:

Individuals with BPD typically struggle with a fragile sense of self and identity instability. They may have a vague or unstable self-image, suffer from a lack of a constant sense of self, and experience feelings of emptiness or not knowing who they actually are.

This identity disruption may lead to difficulty in decision-making, developing objectives, and forming a cohesive sense of personal identity. The persistent quest for identity and the absence of a fixed self-concept might lead to continuing emotions of bewilderment and unhappiness.

5. Self-Harm and Suicidal Behaviors:

Self-harm and suicidal tendencies are important problems related to BPD. The emotional turbulence, severe feelings of emptiness, and problems in dealing with upsetting emotions may prompt persons with BPD to engage in self-harming activities as a maladaptive coping method.

Self-harm may give short respite from emotional anguish or act as a technique to acquire a feeling of control. Additionally, persons with BPD may suffer frequent thoughts of suicide or participate in suicide attempts. The risk of self-harm and suicide behaviors demands constant evaluation and the deployment of appropriate safety measures and assistance.

6. Co-Occurring Disorders:

BPD is commonly accompanied by the existence of co-occurring mental health problems. Common co-occurring illnesses include mood disorders (such as depression and bipolar disorder), anxiety disorders, drug use disorders, eating disorders, and post-traumatic stress disorder (PTSD).

The existence of these co-occurring illnesses may further complicate the diagnosis, treatment, and general management of BPD since they lead to extra obstacles and impairments in functioning.

7. Occupational and Educational Impairment:

The influence of BPD goes beyond personal relationships and emotional well-being to professional and educational areas. Emotional instability, impulsivity, and difficulty in regulating stress might interfere with employment stability, work performance, and career progress.

Individuals with BPD may struggle with keeping jobs, endure numerous job changes or disputes, or have trouble meeting school obligations. The deficits in vocational and educational functioning might lead to financial instability and diminished self-esteem.

8. Social Isolation and Stigma:

The issues associated with BPD may lead to social isolation and a feeling of exclusion. Individuals with BPD may suffer challenges in developing and sustaining social relationships owing to relational issues, emotional instability, and fear of judgment or rejection.

The stigma surrounding BPD may further contribute to feelings of shame, guilt, and a reluctance to seek assistance. The lack of knowledge and awareness of BPD in society might restrict access to adequate care and promote misunderstandings about the disease.

9. Family and Caregiver Burden:
BPD not only affects the persons diagnosed but also has severe repercussions on their families and carers. The emotional intensity, impulsive actions, and relational issues associated with BPD may impose a great load on family members and loved ones.

Caregivers may suffer emotions of powerlessness, frustration, and tiredness as they attempt to manage the obstacles of assisting a person with BPD. Family counseling and support may play a vital role in addressing the effect on families and increasing understanding and appropriate coping methods.

10. Treatment Challenges:
Treating BPD may be difficult and demanding. The multidimensional character of the disease, including emotional

dysregulation, impulsivity, and difficulty in relationships, necessitates integrated and comprehensive therapy. Psychotherapy, such as dialectical behavior therapy (DBT), is the most generally acknowledged and evidence-based treatment for BPD.

However, locating qualified mental health experts that specialize in BPD and have skills in coping with the disease may be problematic. The chronic and persistent nature of BPD demands long-term treatment and care, which may involve counseling, medication, support groups, and psychosocial therapies.

11. Financial Consequences:

The impulsive actions and problems in sustaining steady work might lead to financial ramifications for those with BPD. Reckless spending, employment instability, and financial mismanagement may result in debt, financial instability, and poor relationships with respect to money. These obstacles may further worsen stress and lead to a cycle of financial troubles.

12. Physical Health Complications:

The effect of BPD is not confined to emotional and psychological well-being; it may also have ramifications for physical health. Individuals with BPD may engage in self-harming activities, such as cutting or burning, which may cause physical damage and infections. Additionally, high levels of stress, emotional dysregulation, and impulsive behaviors may lead to physical health difficulties such as sleep disruptions, gastrointestinal disorders, and chronic pain.

13. Interpersonal Conflicts:

The difficulty in controlling emotions, impulsivity, and fear of abandonment may result in frequent interpersonal confrontations for those with BPD. These disputes may develop in personal relationships, friendships, and even in professional situations. The powerful emotions, fast fluctuating moods, and misreading of others' actions or intentions may disrupt relationships, leading to isolation, social disengagement, and a decreased support network.

14. Diminished Quality of Life:

The cumulative effect of the different features of BPD, including emotional instability, impulsivity, relational issues, and identity disorders, may dramatically reduce an individual's overall quality of life.

The ongoing emotional upheaval, fear of abandonment, and difficulty in regulating emotions may hinder those with BPD from feeling stability, meaningful relationships, and a sense of satisfaction. This might result in a chronic feeling of discontent, emptiness, and restricted prospects for personal development and well-being.

15. Risk of Self-Harm and Suicide:

BPD is related to a significant risk of self-harm and suicide. The acute emotional anguish, feelings of emptiness, and difficulty in dealing with uncomfortable emotions may lead to self-harming behaviors as a maladaptive coping method.

Additionally, persons with BPD may suffer recurring thoughts of suicide and participate in suicide attempts. The risk of self-harm and suicide needs constant monitoring, adequate safety measures, and access to mental health assistance.

16. Impact on Caregivers and Loved Ones:

BPD not only impacts persons afflicted with the condition but also has a huge influence on their caretakers and loved ones. Family members and friends may suffer emotional anguish, irritation, and a sense of powerlessness as they negotiate the problems of supporting someone with BPD.

The unexpected mood swings, relational disputes, and extreme emotional responses may strain relationships and create a weight of care.

Borderline Personality Disorder may have wide-ranging and severe implications on people's life, relationships, emotional well-being, and general functioning. Recognizing the effect of BPD is critical for providing appropriate support, therapies, and resources to persons afflicted by the disease.

With early intervention, thorough therapy, and a supporting network, persons with BPD may achieve considerable gains in controlling their symptoms, forming stronger relationships, and living more satisfying lives.

Understanding Borderline Personality Disorder (BPD) is vital for patients, carers, and mental health professionals alike. BPD is a complicated mental health illness characterized by emotional dysregulation, impulsivity, identity issues, and difficulty in interpersonal interactions.

Developing a complete knowledge of BPD is critical for several reasons, including successful treatment, enhanced communication, less stigma, and better overall results.

Importance for Patients

1. Self-Awareness and Validation:

Understanding BPD assists persons diagnosed with the condition to acquire self-awareness and validation. It helps people make meaning of their experiences, emotions, and actions, minimizing self-blame and feelings of isolation. Recognizing that their troubles are related to a diagnosable ailment may bring a feeling of validation and comfort.

2. Empowerment and Personal Growth:

Knowledge about BPD helps people to actively engage in their treatment and recovery path. It enables individuals to learn about evidence-based treatment techniques, coping skills, and self-care practices that may help manage symptoms and enhance overall well-being.

Understanding the illness offers a basis for personal development, as people may identify areas for improvement, build better coping methods, and work towards accomplishing their objectives.

3. Building Resilience and Coping Skills:

Understanding BPD gives people the tools and information to build resilience and develop effective coping abilities. It helps people detect triggers, manage emotional dysregulation, and execute techniques to control emotions and prevent impulsive actions. With improved information, people may make educated choices and adopt healthy methods of handling stress and suffering.

<u>Importance for Caregivers</u>

1. Enhanced Empathy and Support:

Understanding BPD allows caregivers to build empathy and offer educated assistance. It enables people to comprehend the obstacles persons with BPD encounter, such as emotional instability, fear of abandonment, and relational difficulties. With this knowledge, caregivers may react compassionately, validate feelings, and provide necessary assistance without judgment.

2. Improved Communication and Boundaries:

Knowledge of BPD helps enhanced communication between caregivers and persons with the condition. It helps caregivers discover communication patterns, triggers, and emotional needs, leading to more productive and compassionate interactions. Understanding limits and the need for self-care is vital for caregivers to preserve their well-being while offering assistance to their loved ones with BPD.

3. Collaborative Treatment Approach:

Caregivers who understand BPD may actively participate in the treatment process and communicate with mental health specialists. They may contribute vital ideas, share observations, and engage in family therapy sessions or support groups. This collaborative approach boosts the efficacy of therapy and raises the odds of favorable outcomes for patients with BPD.

<u>Importance for Mental Health Professionals</u>

1. Accurate Diagnosis and Treatment Planning:

Having a solid grasp of BPD helps mental health providers to effectively identify the disease and establish specific treatment programs. Recognizing the symptoms, rating their severity, and detecting co-occurring illnesses are critical for offering appropriate therapies and ensuring that patients get the most effective therapy.

2. Evidence-Based Interventions:

Understanding BPD helps mental health providers keep informed on evidence-based therapies and therapy methods. Familiarity with therapies such as dialectical behavior therapy (DBT), schema therapy, and psychopharmacological alternatives helps practitioners to deliver the most relevant interventions for symptom management and long-term rehabilitation.

3. Therapeutic Alliance and Trust:

By understanding BPD, mental health providers may develop a strong therapeutic partnership built on trust and understanding. This connection is crucial for those with BPD, since they may have encountered invalidation, stigma, or judgment in the past. A non-judgmental, empathic, and educated approach promotes a comfortable setting where patients feel understood, affirmed, and supported.

4. Ongoing Support and Relapse Prevention:

BPD needs long-term support and relapse prevention techniques. Mental health specialists who understand the nature of the condition may give continuous therapy, assess progress, and act swiftly in case of relapse. They may teach patients extra coping skills, offer psychoeducation, and treat co-occurring problems, supporting prolonged recovery and well-being.

5. Advocacy and Reducing Stigma:

Understanding BPD helps mental health practitioners to advocate for their patients and create awareness to minimize stigma. By confronting misunderstandings and raising public knowledge of the disease, professionals may contribute to a more compassionate and supportive society.

A complete knowledge of Borderline Personality Disorder is vital for patients, carers, and mental health professionals. It empowers people with BPD, allows caregivers to offer educated support, and helps mental health experts to make accurate diagnoses and successful treatments.

By developing empathy, decreasing stigma, and supporting evidence-based therapies, a shared knowledge of BPD increases the overall well-being and results of persons impacted by the condition.

Chapter 4

HISTORY OF BORDERLINE PERSONALITY DISORDER

Initially, it was suggested that borderline disorder bordered on, or overlapped with schizophrenia, non-schizophrenic psychoses, and neuroses such as anxiety and depressive disorders. Because it seemed to resemble other psychiatric diagnoses, it was commonly believed to be a "wastebasket" diagnosis, lacking in diagnostic precision and validity, and only useful for patients who did not fall clearly into other diagnostic categories.

It also was noticed originally that the disease reacted extremely badly to therapy with psychotherapies, and to drugs when they first became accessible. Unfortunately, a huge percentage of mental health practitioners, especially those in academic settings, are evidently uninformed about the scientific material written on borderline disorder over the last 50 years, nevertheless, assume that this is accurate.

However, a considerable number of research investigations have recently proven that borderline disorder does have diagnostic validity and integrity. Some studies suggest that the condition does not overlap with schizophrenia.

Also, the disorder does appear to be a distinct diagnostic entity, although it co-occurs frequently with other mental disorders such as major depressive and bipolar II disorders, attention deficit hyperactivity disorder (ADHD), substance use disorders, post-traumatic stress disorder (PTSD), and with several other personality disorders.

Most crucially, drugs and specialized types of psychotherapy have been found to be beneficial in the treatment of borderline disorder, so bringing great hope to people who suffer from it, and to their relatives and friends.

The following is a chronological assessment of the significant breakthroughs in our knowledge and treatment of borderline disorder.

Descriptions of persons displaying the signs of borderline disorder were first documented in the medical literature nearly 3000 years ago.

In 1938, the American psychotherapist Adolph Stern wrote one of the most significant pieces to emerge on borderline disorder, then or since. In it, he described in detail most of the symptoms that are now considered diagnostic criteria for the disorder.

He correctly suggested the likely causes of the disorder and listed the fundamental principles of what he believed to be the most effective form of psychotherapy for these patients, many of which are currently in use. Finally, he termed the illness by referring to people with the symptoms he described as "the borderline group."

The psychotherapist Robert Knight, in the 1940s, brought the notions of ego psychology into his definition of borderline disorder. Ego psychology deals with mental mechanisms that allow us to truly see events, properly integrate our ideas and emotions, and generate appropriate reactions to the life around us. He claimed that patients with borderline illnesses exhibit abnormalities in several of these tasks, and he referred to them as "borderline states."

The next important contribution to the discipline was made by the psychotherapist Otto Kernberg. In the 1960s, he proposed that mental disorders were determined by three distinct personality organizations: psychotic; neurotic, and "borderline personality." Kernberg has been a strong proponent of modified psychoanalytic therapy for those patients with borderline disorder who are able to benefit from it.

In 1968, Roy Grinker and his colleagues released findings of the first study undertaken on individuals with the borderline condition, which he referred to as the "borderline syndrome."

The next important development happened in 1975 when John Gunderson and Margaret Singer published a landmark and widely read piece that integrated the relevant, published material on borderline disorder, and presented its primary features. Gunderson then released a particular study tool to promote the proper identification of borderline disorder. This tool enables researchers across the globe to verify the validity and integrity of borderline disorder. Subsequently, borderline personality disorder first appeared in DSM-III as a bona fide psychiatric diagnosis in 1980.

In 1979, John Brinkley, Bernard Beitman, and Robert Friedel provided anecdotal evidence that medications, specifically low doses of neuroleptics (now referred to as antipsychotic agents), are effective in reducing some of the symptoms of borderline disorder.

Friedel's research team published support for this proposal in 1986 in one of the first two placebo-controlled studies of any medication in subjects with borderline disorder. A similar outcome was published in the same publication by Paul Soloff's research team using a different medicine in the same class.

Since then, numerous controlled investigations with comparable drugs have validated and expanded the initial conclusion. In addition, drugs in other classes have been documented to have effectiveness in treating the symptoms of borderline disorder.

In the 1980s, the first of a large number of neuroimaging, biochemical, and genetic research was published suggesting that borderline disorder is linked with biological changes in those brain regions connected to the symptoms of the disease.

In 1991, Marsha Linehan created Dialectical Behavioral Therapy (DBT), a specialized and now well-documented style of psychotherapy for individuals with borderline disorder prone to heightened aggression, and self-injurious conduct and who need and seek repeated, short hospitalizations.

Since then, various techniques of psychotherapy have been created that are particularly suited for the borderline disorder.

More recent breakthroughs in the area of the borderline disorder have been a substantial increase in understanding its prevalence and crippling consequences, its basic nature, and the creation of particular and successful techniques of pharmaceutical and psychological therapy.

Over the last twenty years, a number of lay support and advocacy groups have been created, or extended their involvement, to raise awareness of, information about, and treatment for borderline illness. The most significant ones are the Borderline Personality Disorder Resource Center, the National Education Alliance for Borderline Personality Disorder (NEA-BPD), the Treatment and Research Advancements Association for Personality Disorder (TARA

APD), and the Black Sheep Foundation (BSF).

The missions of these organizations are to increase awareness of borderline disorder and its treatments, provide the names of clinicians skilled in the diagnosis and treatment of the borderline disorder, and provide support and educational opportunities to those suffering from the disorder and their families and friends. In the previous decade, the National Alliance on Mental Illness (NAMI) included BPD in its list of high-priority mental diseases.

For example, the Borderline Personality Disorder Resource Center was designed to assist persons who may have borderline disorder and their families in contacting doctors qualified and experienced in the diagnosis and treatment of borderline disorder and to give other useful information.

The Black Sheep Foundation was recently created to improve public and private research funding devoted particularly to BPD and to remove the stigma associated with the condition. Since 1987, the Brain Research Foundation has granted more than $1 million for research on borderline disorder studies in addition to studies on other mental diseases.

Chapter 5

MYTHS AND MISCONCEPTIONS ABOUT BPD

Borderline Personality Disorder (BPD) is a complicated and frequently misunderstood mental health disorder. Over the years, various myths and beliefs have evolved that lead to stigma, misdiagnosis, and inappropriate treatment.

Addressing these stereotypes is vital for increasing understanding, empathy, and effective support for persons with BPD. Here, we address some of the typical myths and misunderstandings related to BPD:

1. Myth: BPD is untreatable or cannot be controlled.
Reality: BPD is a curable disorder, and with proper therapies and support, people

may enjoy considerable improvements in their symptoms and quality of life. Therapeutic techniques like Dialectical Behavior Therapy (DBT), Cognitive-Behavioral Therapy (CBT), and Schema Therapy have proven successful in helping clients manage BPD symptoms and create better-coping mechanisms.

2. <u>Myth:</u> People with BPD are attention-seeking and manipulative.

<u>**Reality:**</u> This myth originates from misconceptions regarding BPD symptoms, such as self-destructive actions or emotional outbursts. However, these actions are generally a consequence of extreme emotional pain and difficulty in emotion management rather than conscious efforts to attract attention or manipulate people. Individuals with BPD generally want acceptance and connection, and their behaviors may be motivated by a strong fear of abandonment.

3. <u>Myth:</u> BPD is a character's fault or a decision.

<u>Reality:</u> BPD is a recognized mental health condition defined by neurological, psychological, and environmental variables. It is neither a personal failure nor a decision. Like other mental health diseases, BPD is impacted by a mix of genetic, biochemical, and environmental variables. Individuals with BPD require understanding, compassion, and access to adequate treatment.

4. <u>Myth:</u> BPD exclusively affects women.

<u>Reality:</u> BPD is not limited to any gender. While data suggests that more women are diagnosed with BPD compared to males, it is vital to remember that the condition may afflict persons of any gender. The incidence of BPD among males may be underestimated owing to gender biases in diagnosis and social ideals surrounding masculinity.

5. <u>Myth</u>: People with BPD are usually aggressive or violent.

<u>**Reality:**</u> While persons with BPD may feel powerful emotions and demonstrate impulsive actions, they are not fundamentally aggressive or violent. Sensationalized media representations sometimes add to this misperception.

It is vital to note that the majority of persons with BPD are not violent, and their acts are typically motivated by internal misery rather than a desire to hurt others.

6. <u>Myth</u>: BPD is a transitory or transient disorder.

<u>**Reality:**</u> BPD is a long-standing and chronic mental health illness. While people with BPD might have periods of remission and progress, the underlying symptoms and vulnerabilities linked with the condition endure throughout time. Effective therapy and continued support are critical for

controlling BPD symptoms and maintaining long-term well-being.

7. Myth: BPD is the same as Bipolar Disorder.

Reality: BPD is commonly misdiagnosed with Bipolar Disorder owing to the same symptoms of mood swings and emotional dysregulation. However, they are separate illnesses with different diagnostic criteria and therapeutic methods.

BPD generally entails issues in emotion management, self-identity, and interpersonal connections, whereas Bipolar Disorder involves cyclic mood changes between depression and manic episodes.

8. Myth: BPD cannot coexist with other mental health problems.

Reality: Individuals with BPD commonly face comorbid mental health illnesses such as depression, anxiety, drug use disorders, and eating disorders. These co-occurring illnesses might complicate the diagnosis and management of BPD. Addressing both BPD and any concomitant illnesses is critical for complete treatment.

9. Myth: BPD is an uncommon condition.

<u>Reality:</u> BPD is more prevalent than previously recognized. While the prevalence percentages may vary among research, it is believed that roughly 1-2% of the general population may satisfy the criteria for BPD.

This implies that many people and their families are influenced by the condition. Increasing knowledge about the prevalence of BPD helps lessen the isolation and misunderstanding sometimes encountered by people afflicted.

10. Myth: BPD is a product of terrible parenting or a dysfunctional childhood.

<u>Reality:</u> BPD is a complicated condition with numerous origins. While unfavorable childhood events, such as trauma or invalidating situations, might contribute to the development of BPD, it is crucial to note that not all persons who encounter such conditions acquire the illness. Biological variables, genetic predisposition, and a mix of environmental influences also play a crucial role in the development of BPD.

11. Myth: People with BPD cannot maintain solid relationships.

<u>Reality:</u> Individuals with BPD may have meaningful and secure relationships. While the interpersonal issues associated with the condition may make sustaining relationships more challenging, with proper therapy and support, people with BPD can establish healthy relationship patterns.

Building understanding and communication skills may help to more rewarding and stable ties with people.

12. Myth: BPD is an attention-seeking tendency to manipulate people.

Reality: BPD symptoms, such as self-harm or suicidal thoughts, are generally a desperate effort to deal with intense emotional suffering rather than manipulative tactics. People with BPD may struggle with powerful emotions and trouble controlling them, leading to impulsive acts. It is crucial to handle these actions with empathy and compassion, acknowledging the underlying discomfort rather than presuming malicious intent.

13. Myth: BPD is a condition that cannot improve with time.

Reality: While BPD is a chronic disorder, many people see improvements in their symptoms and general functioning over time with adequate therapy and support.

With treatment, coping skills training, and a supportive environment, persons with BPD may learn to control their emotions, develop healthy coping strategies, and lead satisfying lives.

14. Myth: BPD is purely a product of individual faults or inadequacies.

Reality: BPD is not just an issue of individual deficiencies but rather a complex combination of genetic, biochemical, and environmental elements. It is crucial to treat BPD with a compassionate and comprehensive attitude, realizing that persons with the disease may have vulnerabilities and issues that need support and understanding.

15. Myth: BPD is a less severe or less serious mental health issue.

Reality: BPD may have a considerable influence on people's lives, including their relationships, vocational functioning, and general well-being. The emotional intensity, impulsivity, and difficulty in self-regulation may lead to considerable suffering and damage. Recognizing the severity of BPD and providing proper services and support is critical for helping people handle their issues successfully.

By eliminating these myths and misunderstandings, we may create a more accurate and compassionate knowledge of BPD. This knowledge fosters empathy, lowers stigma, and ensures that persons with BPD get the support, validation, and appropriate treatment they need to flourish. It is vital to encourage education and awareness among the general public, healthcare practitioners, and caregivers to develop a more inclusive and supportive society for persons with BPD.

Chapter 6

<u>DIAGNOSIS AND ASSESSMENT</u>

Borderline Personality Disorder (BPD) is a complicated mental health illness that needs thorough and extensive testing for an appropriate diagnosis. Due to the variability of symptoms and the comorbidity with other mental diseases, an in-depth examination is needed.

The diagnosis of BPD is often established by mental health experts, such as psychiatrists, psychologists, or clinical social workers, using defined diagnostic criteria and testing instruments. Here, we cover the process of diagnosing and evaluating BPD:

1. Clinical Interview:

A comprehensive clinical interview is the core of the evaluation procedure for BPD. The physician will engage in a lengthy dialogue with the subject to acquire information about their symptoms, medical history, family history, and psychosocial background. The interview tries to detect the existence of BPD symptoms, estimate the severity, and investigate the effect of these symptoms on many parts of the person's life.

2. Diagnostic Criteria:

The diagnosis of BPD is based on specific criteria defined in the Diagnostic and Statistical Manual of Mental Disorders (DSM-5) issued by the American Psychiatric Association. The DSM-5 criteria for BPD include widespread patterns of instability in interpersonal relationships, self-image, and mood, as well as impulsivity. The presence of at least five of the nine criteria must be satisfied for a diagnosis of BPD.

3. Structured Clinical Interviews:

To boost diagnosis accuracy, doctors may conduct organized clinical interviews particularly intended to diagnose BPD. One regularly used tool is the Structured Clinical Interview for DSM-5 Personality Disorders (SCID-5-PD). It offers a systematic way to diagnose personality disorders, including BPD, and helps maintain consistency and reliability in the diagnosis process.

4. Self-Report Measures:

Self-report measures, including questionnaires and rating scales, may be beneficial in measuring the severity of BPD symptoms and monitoring treatment success. These assessments may concentrate on different components of BPD, including emotional dysregulation, impulsivity, and interpersonal issues.

Examples of self-report assessments include the Borderline Personality Disorder Severity

Index (BPDSI) and the Zanarini Rating Scale for Borderline Personality Disorder (ZAN-BPD).

5. Collateral Information:

Obtaining collateral information from significant people, family members, or close friends may give vital insights into the individual's behavior, functioning, and interpersonal relationships. Collateral information may assist confirm and build upon the self-report information supplied by the subject, adding to a more thorough evaluation.

6. Differential Diagnosis:

Given the overlap of symptoms between BPD and other mental illnesses, it is necessary to undertake a comprehensive differential diagnosis. Conditions such as mood disorders, drug use disorders, other personality disorders, and post-traumatic stress disorder (PTSD) might have comparable symptoms with BPD.

Clinicians must thoroughly analyze the individual's symptoms and history to identify BPD from other disorders and guarantee correct diagnosis and adequate treatment planning.

7. Longitudinal Assessment:

BPD is a complicated and dynamic condition, and symptoms may alter over time. Longitudinal evaluation is vital for following the individual's development, assessing symptom severity, and evaluating treatment effects. Regular follow-up consultations and reassessments enable doctors to make required modifications to the treatment plan and give continuing support.

8. Psychological and Psychometric Assessment:

In addition to the clinical interview and self-report measures, psychological and psychometric testing may give significant information in the diagnosis and assessment of BPD. These evaluations may include:

- **<u>Personality Assessment:</u>** Various personality assessment instruments, such as the Minnesota Multiphasic Personality Inventory (MMPI) or the Millon Clinical Multiaxial Inventory (MCMI), may assist evaluate personality characteristics and uncover particular patterns linked with BPD.

- **<u>Cognitive Assessment:</u>** Assessing cognitive functioning may assist detect cognitive distortions, thinking processes, and cognitive biases typically linked with BPD. This examination may incorporate cognitive tests, such as the Beck Cognitive Insight Scale, or particular assessments addressing cognitive processes associated with impulsivity or emotional control.

- **<u>Emotion Regulation Assessment:</u>** Given the key role of emotional dysregulation in BPD, evaluations that particularly target emotion regulation abilities and challenges might be useful. These evaluations may include self-report measures, such as the Difficulties in Emotion Control Scale (DERS), or structured interviews that examine emotional reactivity and control mechanisms.

9. Cultural Considerations:

When diagnosing and analyzing BPD, it is necessary to include cultural aspects that may impact the presentation of symptoms and the individual's help-seeking behavior. Cultural ideas, values, and conventions may affect the expression of suffering and alter the individual's concept of mental health. Mental health providers should be attentive to cultural diversity, apply a culturally competent approach, and consider the cultural context when evaluating symptoms and developing a diagnosis.

10. Clinical Judgment and Experience:

Diagnosing BPD takes professional judgment and expertise. Mental health practitioners use their experience, understanding of diagnostic criteria, and acquaintance with the intricacies of BPD to reach an appropriate diagnosis. Experience in dealing with persons with BPD helps clinicians to spot trends, analyze the influence of comorbid illnesses, and identify possible problems and strengths in treatment planning.

It is vital to approach the diagnosis and evaluation of BPD with a holistic and comprehensive perspective, incorporating both the subjective experiences of the person and objective diagnostic methods. A complete evaluation helps mental health practitioners to deliver individualized and successful treatment strategies, assist people in managing their symptoms, and promote their overall well-being.

Chapter 7

<u>BPD TREATMENT OPTIONS</u>

Borderline Personality Disorder (BPD) is a complicated mental health disorder characterized by difficulty in managing emotions, unstable self-image, and hard interpersonal connections.

While BPD may offer substantial obstacles, there are different treatment options available that can help patients manage their symptoms, improve their general functioning, and increase their quality of life.

It is vital to remember that therapy for BPD is often long-term and needs a thorough and tailored strategy. Here, we review the numerous therapy options for BPD:

1. Psychotherapy:
Psychotherapy, often known as talk therapy, is a critical component of BPD treatment. Several therapy techniques have been demonstrated to be effective:

a.   Dialectical   Behavior   Therapy (DBT): Developed expressly for BPD, DBT is a comprehensive treatment that involves individual therapy, group skills training, phone coaching, and therapist consulting teams. It focuses on teaching people skills to regulate emotions, increase interpersonal effectiveness, endure suffering, and practice mindfulness.

b.   Cognitive-Behavioral   Therapy (CBT): CBT helps patients recognize and improve negative thinking patterns and behaviors that contribute to BPD symptoms. It focuses on correcting cognitive distortions, creating coping mechanisms, and enhancing problem-solving abilities.

c. **<u>Schema-Focused Therapy:</u>** This method tackles maladaptive patterns or schemas that underlie BPD symptoms. Through treatment, people learn to identify and confront these negative schemas, establish better coping skills, and enhance their self-image.

d. **<u>Mentalization-Based Therapy (MBT):</u>** MBT focuses on strengthening the individual's capacity to comprehend their own and others' mental states. It helps people create more accurate perceptions of interpersonal circumstances, boosting their capacity to manage emotions and build better relationships.

e. **<u>Transference-Focused Psychotherapy (TFP):</u>** TFP strives to help people understand and alter their patterns of connecting to others, especially within the therapeutic interaction. It emphasizes analyzing and working through unsolved problems and challenges in relationships.

2. **Medication:**

While the medicine does not cure BPD, it might be useful in controlling certain symptoms or concomitant diseases. Medications may be administered to alleviate mood instability, sadness, anxiety, or impulsivity.

Commonly recommended drugs include mood stabilizers, antidepressants, antipsychotics, and anti-anxiety meds. It is vital to meet with a psychiatrist who can identify the proper medicine and regularly monitor its efficacy and any negative effects.

3. **Group Therapy:**

Group therapy may be a beneficial supplement to individual treatment for persons with BPD. In a group context, people may connect with others who have similar experiences, exchange ideas, and give support.

Group therapy offers a secure setting to practice interpersonal skills, obtain feedback, and establish a feeling of belonging. Skills-based groups, such as DBT skills training groups, concentrate on teaching particular coping methods and boosting interpersonal efficacy.

4. **Family Therapy:**

Involving family members in the therapy process might be useful for those with BPD. Family therapy strives to promote communication, boost understanding, and establish appropriate boundaries within the family system. It gives a chance to address family dynamics, minimize conflict, and strengthen support networks.

5. <u>Self-Help and Support Groups:</u>

Participating in self-help and support groups may offer those with BPD a feeling of validation, understanding, and a helpful community. These groups frequently follow established programs, such as those based on DBT principles, and may give practical coping skills, peer support, and a platform for sharing experiences.

6. <u>Hospitalization and Intensive Treatment Programs:</u>

In extreme circumstances when persons are in danger of self-harm or suicide, or where symptoms are seriously limiting their everyday functioning, hospitalization or intensive treatment programs may be essential. These programs offer an organized and supportive setting where clients may get intense treatment, crisis management, and stabilization. They strive to protect the individual's safety, treat acute symptoms, and give a more intense degree of care.

7. <u>Complementary Therapies:</u>

Complementary treatments may be effective as adjuncts to established treatment techniques for BPD. These treatments include mindfulness techniques, yoga, art therapy, animal-assisted therapy, and other holistic methods. These approaches may help people control emotions, decrease stress, develop self-awareness, and promote general well-being.

8. <u>Coordinated Care:</u>

Given the complicated nature of BPD, a coordinated and interdisciplinary treatment is typically effective. This may require teamwork between mental health specialists, such as psychiatrists, psychologists, social workers, and primary care doctors. Coordinated care guarantees that therapeutic approaches are coordinated and target the many facets of the individual's well-being.

DBT

Dialectical Behavior Therapy (DBT) is a specialized style of psychotherapy that has been designed exclusively for patients with Borderline Personality Disorder (BPD). It integrates components of cognitive-behavioral therapy, mindfulness techniques, and dialectical philosophy to give a holistic therapeutic strategy.

DBT has been demonstrated to be very helpful in lowering self-destructive behaviors, increasing emotion control, and improving general functioning in patients with BPD. Let's investigate DBT in more detail:

DBT was established in the late 1980s by psychologist Dr. Marsha M. Linehan. It was first intended to address the high-risk behaviors and emotional dysregulation often encountered by patients with BPD. DBT is founded on the idea of dialectics, which stresses achieving a balance between acceptance and change. The treatment is organized, time-limited, and often offered in a mix of individual therapy, group skills training, phone coaching, and therapist consulting teams.

Components of DBT

a. **Individual Therapy:** The individual therapy component of DBT focuses on helping people recognize and alter harmful behaviors, develop skills to regulate uncomfortable emotions, and address particular issues they confront in everyday life. The therapist works jointly with the person to develop objectives and aims for therapy.

b. **Group Skills Training:** The group skills training component entails attending weekly group sessions where participants acquire particular skills to increase their capacity to manage emotions, endure discomfort, effectively communicate, and navigate interpersonal relationships. The techniques taught include mindfulness, mood management, distress tolerance, and interpersonal effectiveness.

c. **<u>Phone Coaching:</u>** DBT incorporates phone coaching, which enables people to get support and advice from their therapist outside of regular treatment sessions. This helps people use the skills they have learned in real-life circumstances and handle emergencies successfully.

d. **<u>Therapist Consultation Team:</u>** Therapist consultation teams comprise DBT therapists that meet frequently to give support and consultation to one another. These sessions assist therapists maintain their own efficacy and guarantee that they give the best possible treatment to their clients.

3. **Core Principles of DBT:**

a. **Dialectics:** DBT is built on the idea of dialectics, which stresses achieving a balance between acceptance and change. It encourages people to accept themselves and their existing situations while simultaneously striving towards change and personal progress.

b. **Mindfulness:** Mindfulness is a crucial component of DBT and entails paying attention to the present moment without judgment. By cultivating mindfulness skills, people may examine and accept their thoughts, feelings, and sensations, which assists in emotion management and minimizes impulsive actions.

c. **Emotion Regulation:** BPD is generally characterized by strong and quickly fluctuating emotions. DBT helps people gain abilities to recognize, comprehend, and manage their emotions successfully. These abilities include detecting emotional triggers, enhancing good feelings, and lowering emotional susceptibility.

d. **<u>Distress Tolerance:</u>** Individuals with BPD generally suffer from distress tolerance, leading to impulsive or self-destructive actions. DBT offers strategies to manage upsetting circumstances without turning to destructive actions. These abilities comprise diversion methods, self-soothing strategies, and accepting reality.

e. **<u>Interpersonal Effectiveness:</u>** Difficulties in interpersonal connections are typical in BPD. DBT helps clients with strategies to enhance communication, create boundaries, express their needs, and build healthy and rewarding relationships.

4. Effectiveness of DBT:

Research has repeatedly established the efficacy of DBT in lowering self-destructive behaviors, suicide attempts, and hospitalizations among patients with BPD. DBT has also demonstrated good benefits in lowering feelings of despair, anxiety, and rage. Furthermore, DBT has been modified for use with different groups and mental health issues, including drug use disorders, eating disorders, and post-traumatic stress disorder (PTSD).

5. Adapting DBT for Various Settings: DBT has been developed to fit diverse therapeutic settings and groups. Variations of DBT include modified DBT for adolescents, DBT for substance use disorders (DBT-SUD), and DBT for couples. These adjustments guarantee that the ideas and abilities of DBT may be successfully applied to varied therapeutic groups.

DBT has changed the treatment of Borderline Personality Disorder by offering an organized and evidence-based approach to handling the various issues associated with the disease.

Through a mix of individual treatment, group skills training, phone coaching, and therapist consultation teams, persons with BPD may acquire effective techniques to control their emotions, build stronger interpersonal connections, and eventually enhance their overall well-being.

Chapter 8

NATURAL THERAPY ALTERNATIVES FOR BPD

Borderline personality disorder (BPD) is a complicated mental health illness characterized by fluctuating emotions, self-image, and relationships. While BPD is normally treated with counseling and drugs, some patients may also investigate natural treatment methods to supplement their standard treatment strategy.

It's crucial to remember that natural therapies should not substitute professional medical advice or prescription medications. However, some natural treatments may give extra assistance and increase general well-being for those with BPD. Here are some natural therapy methods that have been recommended or examined in connection to BPD:

1. **<u>Mindfulness & Meditation:</u>** Mindfulness activities, including meditation and deep breathing exercises, may assist persons with BPD to acquire more awareness of their emotions and thoughts. Mindfulness-based treatments, such as Dialectical Behavior Therapy (DBT), have demonstrated encouraging benefits in lowering symptoms of BPD and promoting emotional control.

2. **<u>Exercise:</u>** Engaging in regular physical exercise has been demonstrated to have several advantages for mental health. Exercise encourages the production of endorphins, which are natural mood enhancers, and may help relieve tension and anxiety. It may help enhance self-esteem and body image, which are sometimes issues for those with BPD.

3. **<u>Herbal Supplements:</u>** Certain herbal supplements have been examined for their possible usefulness in controlling BPD symptoms. St. John's Wort, for example, has been long used for mood disorders and may help decrease symptoms of despair, anxiety, and irritability. However, it's crucial to contact a healthcare expert before taking any herbal supplements, since they may mix with pharmaceuticals and may not be suited for everyone.

4. **<u>Omega-3 Fatty Acids:</u>** Omega-3 fatty acids, present in fish oil and some plant sources like flaxseed, have been examined for their possible impact on mental health. Some study shows that omega-3 supplementation may help lessen depressive symptoms and enhance emotional stability in patients with BPD.

While additional research is required to provide unambiguous recommendations, incorporating omega-3-rich foods in your diet or taking supplements under physician supervision may be worth exploring.

5. **<u>Acupuncture:</u>** Acupuncture, an ancient Chinese medicinal treatment, involves putting small needles into particular spots on the body. It has been examined as a complementary therapy for several mental health problems, including BPD.

While the data is limited, several studies show that acupuncture may help lower anxiety, despair, and general suffering in persons with BPD. It's crucial to identify a competent and licensed acupuncturist if you decide to explore this therapy option.

6. **<u>Yoga and Tai Chi:</u>** Yoga and Tai Chi are mind-body disciplines that include physical movements, breathing exercises, and meditation. These techniques have been demonstrated to relieve stress, increase emotional well-being, and develop self-awareness. Engaging in frequent yoga

or Tai Chi lessons may create a feeling of tranquility and assist those with BPD regulate their emotional states.

7. **<u>Supportive connections and Peer Support:</u>** Building and sustaining supportive connections is vital for those with BPD. Engaging in therapy groups, support groups, or seeking peer support may bring validation, understanding, and a feeling of community. Peer support groups, such as those established by mental health organizations or online communities, may give vital insights and coping skills shared by persons with comparable experiences.

8. **<u>Aromatherapy:</u>** Aromatherapy includes utilizing essential oils to enhance relaxation and well-being. Certain smells, such as lavender, chamomile, or bergamot, are recognized for their relaxing qualities. Incorporating aromatherapy into your daily routine via diffusers, massage oils, or

scented candles may help decrease anxiety and generate a feeling of calm.

9. **<u>Art Therapy:</u>** Art therapy gives a creative medium for self-expression and emotional inquiry. Engaging in different creative forms, such as painting, sketching, or sculpting, may help persons with BPD manage their emotions, boost self-awareness, and build better coping skills. Art therapy may be explored alone or as part of an organized therapeutic program.

10. **<u>Herbal Teas:</u>** Certain herbal teas have relaxing effects that may help relieve anxiety and encourage relaxation. Examples include chamomile tea, lemon balm tea, or passionflower tea. Drinking a warm cup of herbal tea before sleep or during times of heightened stress may be a relaxing habit that assists in controlling mental discomfort.

11. **Massage and Bodywork:** Massage therapy and bodywork methods, such as Swedish massage, deep tissue massage, or reflexology, may induce relaxation, ease muscular tension, and reduce stress. These activities may have a soothing impact on the body and mind, helping persons with BPD find respite from emotional and physical symptoms.

12. **Light treatment:** Light treatment, also known as phototherapy, includes exposure to intense artificial light to regulate mood and relieve symptoms of depression. While it's usually used for seasonal affective disorder, several studies have suggested its potential advantages in treating depressive symptoms in patients with BPD. Light therapy should be used under the advice of a healthcare practitioner.

13. **Sleep Hygiene**: Establishing a regular sleep regimen and practicing proper sleep hygiene may dramatically improve overall

well-being. Prioritizing adequate sleep and having a pleasant sleep environment, such as following a regular sleep schedule, minimizing screen time before bed, and adopting a soothing bedtime ritual, may help stabilize mood and promote emotional regulation.

14. **<u>Dietary Considerations:</u>** While there is no special BPD diet, adopting a well-balanced diet that includes whole foods, fruits, vegetables, lean meats, and healthy fats may help general mental and physical health. Some persons with BPD may find that limiting excessive coffee, alcohol, and processed foods might help lessen mood fluctuations and enhance their well-being.

15. **<u>Journaling:</u>** Keeping a diary may be a great tool for those with BPD to monitor their feelings, identify triggers, and gain insight into their thoughts and actions. Writing down thoughts, emotions, and

experiences consistently may foster self-reflection, create a sense of relief, and aid in spotting trends or progress in controlling symptoms.

Remember, it's crucial to contact a mental health professional before beginning any natural therapy choices, as they can give assistance targeted to your unique requirements and ensure they correspond with your overall treatment plan.

Additionally, a holistic strategy that combines natural remedies with therapy and medication, as recommended by a healthcare expert, is typically the most effective method to control BPD symptoms and enhance overall well-being.

Chapter 9

<u>WORK AND BPD</u>

Handling borderline personality disorder (BPD) at work may provide distinct issues for both persons with BPD and their coworkers. The office environment may elicit significant emotions and interpersonal challenges, compromising job performance and relationships. However, with education, support, and appropriate techniques in place, it is feasible to manage BPD well at work. Here are thorough instructions for addressing BPD in the workplace:

1. **<u>Educate Yourself and Raise Awareness:</u>** Educate yourself and coworkers about BPD to create understanding and minimize stigma. Share information on the illness, its symptoms, and successful treatment techniques.

Promote empathy and promote open communication to establish a healthy work atmosphere.

2. **Seek therapy and Maintain Therapy:** Individuals with BPD should prioritize their mental health and seek professional therapy. Engage in treatment, such as dialectical behavior therapy (DBT) or cognitive-behavioral therapy (CBT), to develop coping skills and emotional management strategies. Consistently attending therapy sessions and sticking to recommended treatment plans may help improve control of symptoms in the workplace.

3. **Communicate with Your Supervisor:** If you feel comfortable, try addressing your BPD diagnosis with your supervisor or HR department. This talk may help develop a supportive and understanding work environment. Discuss any workplace accommodations or

adaptations that may boost your productivity and well-being, such as flexible scheduling or workspace modifications.

4. **<u>Manage Stress and Emotional Regulation:</u>** BPD symptoms might worsen under stressful conditions. Learn and practice stress management strategies, such as deep breathing exercises, mindfulness, and meditation, to control emotions. Taking small breaks during the workday and participating in relaxing activities might also assist maintain emotional equilibrium.

5. **<u>Establish Clear limits:</u>** Setting and maintaining limits is key for controlling BPD in the workplace. Clearly explain your requirements, restrictions, and expectations to coworkers and managers. Respectfully refuse excessive responsibilities or tasks that may overwhelm you. Establishing limits improves self-care and minimizes burnout.

6. **<u>Create Coping techniques:</u>** Identify and create coping techniques that work for you in managing BPD symptoms at work. This might involve maintaining a diary to process feelings, practicing grounding skills during stressful periods, or employing self-soothing hobbies like listening to peaceful music or participating in a creative outlet. Experiment with several ways to determine what helps you remain focused and centered.

7. **<u>Enhance Communication Skills:</u>** Effective communication is vital for managing relationships in the workplace. Focus on active listening, assertiveness, and expressing your requirements clearly and politely. Practice communicating issues or disputes in a non-confrontational way. Developing good communication skills may assist negotiate tricky circumstances and establish great workplace connections.

8. **<u>Build Supportive connections:</u>** Cultivate supportive connections with coworkers who are sympathetic and compassionate. Identify folks that you trust and can confide in when required. Having a dependable support system at work may give a feeling of validation and understanding.

9. **<u>Manage Impulsive actions:</u>** BPD may be accompanied with impulsive actions that may hinder job performance. Implement measures to regulate impulsive inclinations, such as building a decision-making process that includes taking a pause before acting, receiving input from trusted colleagues before making crucial choices, or channeling impulsive energy into productive work.

10. **<u>Develop Effective Stress Management Techniques:</u>** Find healthy strategies to handle stress and anxiety in the job. Engage in frequent physical activity, such as walking or stretching, during

breaks. Practice self-care outside of work hours, including hobbies, relaxing methods, and spending time with supportive friends or family.

11. **<u>Practice Self-Advocacy:</u>** Advocate for your needs in the workplace, including any adjustments that may promote your well-being. Communicate freely with supervisors about any issues you have and work jointly to discover solutions. Be proactive in seeking help and services available via your workplace's Employee Assistance Program (EAP) or mental health programs.

12. **<u>Maintain job-Life Balance:</u>** Balancing job responsibilities with self-care is vital for managing BPD efficiently. Prioritize self-care activities outside of work, such as indulging in hobbies, spending time with loved ones, and obtaining proper rest. Establishing boundaries between work and

personal life helps reduce burnout and enhances general well-being.

13. **<u>Seek Support Outside of Work:</u>** Consider joining in support groups or obtaining treatment outside of work. These tools give a safe area to discuss issues, get help, and connect with others who may have similar experiences. Support outside of work might complement the support received inside the workplace.

14. **<u>Stay Committed to Treatment:</u>** Consistency in attending therapy sessions, taking prescribed medicines, and implementing self-care skills is crucial. Maintain open contact with your mental health specialists, changing therapy as required to manage symptoms successfully. Stay dedicated to your treatment plan to guarantee your well-being and success at work.

15. **<u>Foster a Positive Work Environment:</u>** Contribute to a positive work environment by fostering polite dialogue, collaboration, and understanding. Lead by example in displaying empathy and compassion towards coworkers. Foster a corporate culture that emphasizes mental health and well-being for all workers.

16. **<u>Develop Time Management Skills:</u>** Individuals with BPD may struggle with time management and organizing. Develop techniques to successfully manage your time and prioritize responsibilities. Break major projects into smaller, achievable tasks and establish reasonable timeframes. Utilize calendars, to-do lists, or digital productivity tools to keep organized and on track.

17. **<u>Implement Stress-Relief tactics:</u>** Incorporate stress-relief tactics into your work routine to control anxiety and avoid excessive feelings. This might involve taking brief pauses during the day to participate in

deep breathing exercises, stretching, or practicing mindfulness. Find what works best for you and apply these tactics into your everyday work routine.

18. **Address confrontation Appropriately:** BPD may make persons more sensitive to criticism and prone to confrontation. When confronted with disputes at work, aim to handle them in a productive and aggressive way. Practice active listening, explore diverse views, and voice your issues calmly and politely. If required, employ a mediator or supervisor to assist promote settlement.

19. **Seek input and Constructive Criticism:** Request input from superiors or coworkers on your performance. Constructive criticism may help you find areas for development and professional progress. Be receptive to critique, and consider it as a chance for personal improvement. This proactive approach

indicates your desire to progress and may favorably improve your professional relationships.

20. **<u>Develop a Support System:</u>** Surround yourself with a supportive network of coworkers, friends, or mentors who understand and appreciate your path. Share your experiences and difficulties with folks who may give insight and support. Having a support system inside the workplace may give a feeling of affirmation and assist you negotiate challenging circumstances.

21. **<u>Practice Self-Reflection and Self-Awareness:</u>** Cultivate self-awareness by reflecting on your emotions, triggers, and behavioral patterns at work. Pay attention to any negative or self-sabotaging ideas and confront them with more balanced and realistic thinking. Regularly check in with yourself to evaluate your emotional

well-being and make any required modifications to your self-care regimen.

22. **<u>Utilize Accommodations and Workplace services:</u>** If your workplace has accommodations or services for those with mental health disorders, take advantage of them. This might include flexible work hours, dedicated quiet rooms, or access to an Employee Assistance Program (EAP) for mental health assistance. Familiarize yourself with these resources and employ them as required to support your well-being.

23. **<u>Monitor and Manage limits:</u>** BPD may make it tough to create and maintain limits. Practice self-awareness and evaluate your interactions with coworkers to ensure you are respecting their limits and your own. Seek guidance from a therapist or counselor to build healthy boundary-setting skills and negotiate interpersonal dynamics in the workplace.

24. __Celebrate Your Successes:__ Acknowledge and celebrate your successes at work, no matter how minor they may appear. Recognize your talents, achievements, and development. Rewarding yourself for your hard work and successes may enhance your self-esteem and motivation, boosting your overall job satisfaction.

25. __Advocate for Mental Health Awareness:__ Consider being an advocate for mental health awareness in the workplace. Share your experiences and views with colleagues, join in mental health projects or committees, or contribute to conversations on fostering a psychologically healthy work environment. By increasing awareness, you may assist build a more supportive and inclusive workplace atmosphere for everyone.

Remember, managing BPD at work is a constant process that includes self-care, self-awareness, and continuing assistance. Implementing these tactics may help you handle workplace problems, preserve your well-being, and prosper in your working life. Reach out to mental health specialists, support groups, or trustworthy persons for further direction and help as required.

Chapter 10

<u>SUPPORTING PEOPLE WITH BPD</u>

People with borderline personality disorder (BPD) tend to have considerable difficulty with relationships, particularly with those closest to them. Their unpredictable mood swings, furious outbursts, chronic abandonment concerns, and impulsive and illogical actions may leave loved ones feeling powerless, mistreated, and off balance.

Partners and family members of persons with BPD typically characterize the relationship as an emotional roller coaster with no end in sight. You may feel that you're at the mercy of your loved one's BPD symptoms—trapped until you leave the relationship or the individual makes measures to obtain treatment. But you have more power than you believe.

You may modify the connection by regulating your own responses, creating strong boundaries, and enhancing communication between you and your loved one. There's no magic cure but with the correct therapy and support, many individuals with BPD can and do get better and their relationships can become more secure and meaningful. In fact, patients with the greatest support and stability at home tend to exhibit changes sooner than those whose relationships are more chaotic and insecure.

Whether it's your spouse, parent, child, sibling, friend, or other loved one with BPD, you can enhance both the relationship and your own quality of life, even if the person with BPD isn't ready to admit the issue or seek therapy.

Supporting persons with borderline personality disorder (BPD) takes patience, understanding, and a sympathetic attitude. BPD may profoundly impair an individual's emotions, relationships, and general well-being. Here are some thorough practices and ideas for assisting persons with BPD:

1. **Educate Yourself:** Gain a full awareness of BPD by educating yourself on the disorder. Learn about its symptoms, causes, and treatment options. Familiarize yourself with the issues experienced by persons with BPD, such as emotional instability, fear of abandonment, and trouble regulating emotions. By knowing the nature of the condition, you can build empathy and react to their needs more effectively.

2. **Encourage Professional treatment:** Encourage persons with BPD to seek professional treatment. A mental health

expert, such as a psychiatrist, psychologist, or therapist, may make a diagnosis, suggest suitable treatment choices, and teach coping techniques. Help them contact a therapist who specializes in BPD or dialectical behavior therapy (DBT), since these therapeutic techniques have proven success in controlling BPD symptoms.

3. **<u>Be Non-judgmental:</u>** Individuals with BPD frequently endure self-stigma and criticism from others owing to the powerful feelings and actions linked with the condition. Offer non-judgmental support and understanding. Avoid condemning or humiliating them for their hardships. Instead, concentrate on recognizing their feelings and emotions, which may develop a sense of safety and trust.

4. **<u>Practice Active Listening:</u>** Listening actively and attentively is vital when assisting someone with BPD. Give them your complete attention, keep eye contact,

and show real interest in what they are saying. Reflect their emotions and ideas to display understanding and empathy. Avoid interrupting or ignoring their feelings, even though you may find their responses tough to grasp.

5. **<u>Set Boundaries:</u>** Boundaries are vital when assisting someone with BPD. Clearly convey your limitations and expectations in a courteous and sensitive way. Encourage children to accept responsibility for their actions while providing a safe and supportive atmosphere. Setting limits may help develop a feeling of security and encourage better relationships.

6. **<u>Validate Their Emotions:</u>** Validation is a vital strategy in aiding those with BPD. Acknowledge and validate their feelings, even though you may not entirely understand or agree with their viewpoint. Let them know that their sentiments are genuine and that you are there to support

them. Validation helps relieve emotional pain and develops a feeling of acceptance and understanding.

7. **<u>Encourage Healthy Coping techniques:</u>** Individuals with BPD may turn to poor coping techniques, such as self-harm or impulsive actions, to manage their high emotions. Encourage and encourage the development of healthy coping methods.

This might involve participating in mindfulness exercises, practicing deep breathing methods, writing, indulging in creative activities, or getting help from a therapist or support group. Promote good alternatives to self-destructive behaviour.

8. **<u>Be Mindful of Abandonment Issues:</u>** Fear of abandonment is a major issue for those with BPD. Be cognizant of this fear and seek to maintain constant and trustworthy assistance. Avoid abrupt or

extreme changes in your degree of participation, and talk freely about any changes or interruptions in your relationship. Reassure them of your dedication and availability within the parameters you have established.

9. **<u>Foster a Supportive Network:</u>** Encourage the person with BPD to create a supportive network of friends, family, or support groups. Peer support may give further understanding, empathy, and affirmation. Help them locate services such as BPD support groups, online forums, or therapy groups where they may connect with others who have similar experiences.

10. **<u>Take Care of Yourself:</u>** Supporting someone with BPD may be emotionally exhausting. It is crucial to prioritize self-care and create limits to preserve your own well-being. Seek help from friends, family, or experts to process your own feelings and difficulties. Remember that you cannot fully

hold the burden of their healing or manage their emotions totally on your own.

11. **Encourage Self-Help and Self-Advocacy:** Empower persons with BPD to take an active part in their own rehabilitation. Support their attempts to participate in self-help tactics, such as reading self-help books, attending seminars or webinars, and performing self-care activities. Encourage them to advocate for their needs in therapy and other healthcare settings, helping them build good communication skills.

12. **Be Patient and Resilient:** Supporting someone with BPD may be tough, since improvement may be sluggish and setbacks may occur. Practice patience and resilience. Celebrate their triumphs, no matter how minor, and provide support at tough times. Remind yourself that rehabilitation is a process, and regular support may make a significant impact in their life.

13. **<u>Practice Effective Communication:</u>**
Effective communication is vital when assisting someone with BPD. Use straightforward and direct communication, avoiding unclear or imprecise remarks. Be cautious of your tone and body language, since persons with BPD might be sensitive to perceived criticism or rejection. Encourage open and honest discussion, so both sides may share their views and emotions without judgment.

14. **<u>Encourage DBT Skills Training:</u>**
Dialectical Behavior Therapy (DBT) is a very successful therapy strategy for BPD. Encourage persons with BPD to engage in DBT skills training, which focuses on developing emotional regulation, distress tolerance, interpersonal effectiveness, and mindfulness. Support their participation in learning and practicing these skills, since they may have a substantial influence on

their capacity to regulate emotions and relationships.

15. **<u>Crisis Management strategy:</u>** Work with the person with BPD and their mental health practitioner to build a crisis management strategy. This plan specifies measures to be followed during times of heightened distress or probable self-harm activities. It might contain emergency contacts, coping skills, and specific steps to assure their safety. Familiarize yourself with the plan and be prepared to follow it if a crisis develops.

16. **<u>Encourage Healthy Lifestyle Choices:</u>** Promote a healthy lifestyle that includes frequent exercise, a balanced diet, and adequate sleep. Encourage the person with BPD to participate in activities that promote self-care and well-being, such as hobbies, relaxation methods, and participating in social interactions. These

lifestyle choices may help to their general stability and resilience.

17. **<u>Foster Independence and Autonomy:</u>** Support the development of independence and autonomy in persons with BPD. Encourage children to make choices, take responsibility for their behaviors, and strive towards their own objectives. Help them recognize their talents and create confidence in their skills. Empowering persons with BPD to become more self-reliant may boost their feeling of self-worth and minimize dependency on external validation.

18. **<u>Be Flexible and Adaptable:</u>** Individuals with BPD may suffer swings in mood, needs, and preferences. Be flexible and adaptive in your assistance, realizing that their requirements may vary over time. Remain open to altering limits and techniques as required while preserving your personal well-being. Flexibility in

assisting them may build the trust and relationship between both parties.

19. **Encourage Healthy Relationships:** Help persons with BPD form and maintain healthy relationships. Offer help on creating boundaries, effective communication, and conflict resolution skills. Encourage them to surround themselves with supportive and empathetic folks who can contribute positively to their mental well-being.

20. **Appreciate gains and Resilience**: Recognize and appreciate the gains achieved by persons with BPD, no matter how modest. Acknowledge their efforts, perseverance, and the measures they take towards their rehabilitation. This positive reinforcement may enhance their confidence, drive, and feeling of success.

21. **Seek Support for Yourself:** Supporting someone with BPD may be emotionally exhausting. It's vital to seek

help for oneself. Consider attending therapy sessions, joining support groups for family and friends of persons with BPD, or getting help from mental health specialists who specialize in BPD. Taking care of your own well-being helps you to give greater assistance and keep a good balance in your own life.

Remember, helping someone with BPD involves patience, understanding, and continual effort. Each individual's experience with BPD is unique, therefore it's crucial to customize your assistance to their personal requirements. Encourage professional aid, encourage healthy communication and limits, and establish a supportive atmosphere that recognizes their development and resilience.

www.ingramcontent.com/pod-product-compliance
Lightning Source LLC
Chambersburg PA
CBHW070948260726
48661CB00003B/1171